The Night You Were Born

Bronmin Shumway

Buckman Publishing LLC
PO Box 14247
Portland OR 97293
buckmanpublishing.com

THE NIGHT YOU WERE BORN/ Bronmin Shumway
ISBN: 9781967058013

Book design by Rich Perin

Cover art: *L'Extase* by Jean-Claude Gaugy (with additional acknowledgments to proprietor Michelle Gaugy)

Editorial assistance by Brian Brodeur

Patronage by Stan and Brandy Shumway and Dale King

With gratitude to Kirk Sonnenberg

Poems in this book originally appeared in the following: *Damn Intellectuals, Empowerment4Women, MotherVerse, X Magazine, The Green Muse,* and *LanguageandCulture.net*

Greetings from Portland, Oregon.

Dedicated to Landon

The
Night
You
Were
Born

Contents

Note from the author:

As a result of my inability or unwillingness to separate the chuckle from the sob, the everyday from the grief-filled, there is in *The Night You Were Born* what the poet Brian Brodeur has aptly described as a "playful wackiness that belies a heartfelt current underneath." I think of the poems in this collection as the stuff you might share with a close friend during the best of conversations—when all of one's humanness is welcome under one quilt, and better for being shared. In *The Night You Were Born*, you will find poems of friendship, broader relationships, youth, parenthood, middle and old age, the workplace, the political, and music. You will find the poems talk to one another; you will find conversation. In my mind, *The Night You Were Born* celebrates you, the reader, just for being here. May you find a close friend or two within the pages.

~Bronmin Shumway

Her Laughter

———

Breaks, like a snap pea.

Cleats

———

There is nowhere, nothing on the green
that Margaret hasn't been or seen.
Worse than any gopher, a real criminal—she doesn't think
of the plaid-clad men, the sad-mad men
whose balls she'll sink.

"Kids," they decide. "Boys," examining the foot holes,
their slim, thin shape,
small enough to be petite.
But they were made by Margaret's feet.

Run, Maggie, run! It's midnight.
Nobody's father
would stop to believe
it was you, Magpie, who interrupted his swing.

At the Bus Stop

———

I was reading a poem by Raúl Salinas
when two Chicanos in a worn-out pickup
stopped and shouted, "You need a ride, *guera*?"
I shook my head and looked back at the page
as they made kissing/sucking
noises and pulled away.

Little Ugly

———

If at the end,
your eyes are like veils,

may they draw on me.

If your face is a shroud,
may it hide my own

at the end.

But if you wake,
I will tell you, friend,

I love you NOW—
not just for who you

could have been
in the sun.

Well-being Check, 100 Merryman Street

The oven light was left on, and one of the burners too,
and all of my emotions, hapless mouths gagged,
farther towards the distance crept
out and were cold.

Night Picnic

This is what I enjoy most: a fat lime slice
stuffed into cold beer, the voice
of a friend—your voice
and mine, tonight,
the slow feathers of summer,
both heavy and light.

Ho! It is my birthday.
There is a banquet laid out for every love.

Ho! It is the new year.
I am in Italy now. The men are rowing.

Oh, moon. Oh, ingot. Oh tuck-me-in-at-night.
This is what I enjoy most: cold beer
and a fat lime slice.

American Day

─────

Slow as a wheel
stops,
slow as a butcher's
chops,

slow as the lady
arranges
her ink-filled dots,

the day shrinks.

Ascending

─────

Ascending isn't a trick;
it's what you do when you're born with wings,
and you were born with wings.

The Kite

———

You have to stand with your back to the wind
and let it blow past you,
if you want to fly a kite.

A good enough breeze has to come along,
and you have to run with it,
hold it at the bridle point,
then let the line out
if you want it to fly.

Fly, love.

I will anchor you, back to the wind,
hair in my face. It's a rush!—

I will listen for the right whispers.
I will trek for miles,
arms extended,
ready to let the line out
at the right time.

That's a promise.

Secret? -I have scissors
in my pocket.
I've been carrying them for a while, or all along.

I will un-hope and hope, now or never,
you and the blue sky

run off together.

Today

———

I have breasts to bear
and hips that move
and hair on my head
that wants to be pulled.

Tomorrow

———

I have breasts that sag
and hips that hurt
and a hair on my chin
that falls into my soup.

Beard

Millicent wasn't born with a beard
but it grew in good.
Now she has to go to Celia's Wax-n-Weave
to get it peeled off.

They do a nice job. For three weeks in a row,
clean as an egg, her chinny-chin-chin
quite ordinary, ready-to-wear
doesn't bother anybody, doesn't make young girls shriek
or men groan.

It's the fourth week that's the problem. It just comes in!

And even though the girl at Celia's is nice,
takes out the wax, and says, each time,
"This'll be warm, now,"
Millicent doesn't like to go, gets embarrassed.

They aren't altogether ugly, the hairs. A bit like cat whiskers,
if you want to split them like that.

Sleeping Over at Diane's

———

Awake, but in a dream,
we ate blueberry ice-cream.
The blueberries were whole.
We were on a roll.
We couldn't get enough
of that sweet stuff.

Smoke

———

Clouds of

in the

with her

and I

drag . . .

Second Base

—————

The first boy who tried to feel me up
was old enough to be a man.
He did it in the bishop's van.

The second who tried to feel me up,
he was the bishop's son.
I crossed my arms until he was done.

The third—well, I don't remember him.
I guess I must have let him do it.
I guess I must have thought,

Let him worry about God, for once.

Desire

—————

For the stubbed paw at the door,
the hunger, tapping,

the wing of the bee at 3:00 AM,
bzzt! in the sconce,

we mourn alike—

knowing what it is to want in,
to want out.

The Fire Pits

———

It's my first time in a helicopter.
We circle the campsite,
and I can't help but notice the fire pits
in the early morning, still smoking.

From here, the campgrounds look like
sleeping leopards, spotted.

This is how it might look
when the body dies, I think,
and I think of a woman with cigarette burns
in her skin.

I know that for most, it wouldn't be a first instinct—
conjuring the image of a woman like an ashtray
from a helicopter
on a beautiful morning like today's.

But I've seen her. And once you've seen her,
you can't forget her.

Her purr is an ache that you could hear
if you could hear an orange peel.

Don't worry. She's fine.
She stares at me from the ash heaps.
She says, "Don't worry."

I tell the pilot to turn around.
It's not as if I'm prone to morbid fascinations;
it's just that I fixed my lipstick
in a mirror once that looked like this.

Sword-lily

———

Like long stems
in a short vas,
you bend for that
which can't possibly
contain you.

May you bloom enough
to be seen
before the weight
of servitude
claims you,

oh gladiola mine.

Electroshock

———

You have been snaked and drained; you are a bathtub.
You have been thrown down the chute, an empty box.
Hollowed out like a tooth, carved up like a squash.
O mind of mine, so pish and so posh!

Someone, please—tell me: What *is* my name?

Swoon

Under the first front,
at last,

I wake to find your poem,
airy and intact.

Intact, meaning, it is whole.
It is nearly a person, the way it breathes.

Good morning! Good morning!
So cold. So clean.

For D-Madness, the Blind-But-Still-Can-See Piscean Badass
March 4, 1999

On our mutual birthday, he smacked
a wall until it sang. Dwayne can do
just about anything, and I mean
any *thang*.

Thumps the bass guitar like a fish
fidgeting on the line. Dwayne wears
his ears on his eyes; out of six
senses—he's got nine.

Dwayne's a good friend of mine.

The Night You Were Born

―――

The night you were born
the lights went out in New York City.

The sugar beets sweetened in the field.
A mountain lion found its feet.

A poet wrote, "The moon kissed the rafters."
And then, "The weather of life turned."

And in Los Tuxtlas, a fig shook loose,
bigger than a Japanese pear.

Eggs

―――

What to do without eggs?
Do I perform a dance?
Do I pretend that I'm not a drunken asshole
at 6:00 AM?

I need eggs,
to fry their little orange heads,
little pumpkins.

Pumpkin, Mama's sorry.
I'll do better tomorrow.
I'll be better tomorrow.

What to do without eggs?
I have no legs.

Wisdom

———

Grandpa, why do you put pennies in a jar?
- So I know where they are.

More Wisdom

———

Grandma, why are you staying up so late?
- That's what it takes to put food on your plate.

Nothing Good Happens After Midnight

———

I'm sorry.
I didn't mean to
tiptoe
through the dark
and step out
and step out
and step out

so that the pervert
neighbor,
had he woken
at 2:33 AM
and gone to his window

would have seen me
raise my nightgown
to my knees

so that it billowed
yes, like a cloud,
and no, Mother, I wasn't afraid.

Liberté at Christiane's

———

Your mom let us put jam on *pain perdu*,
and syrup, too. Sugar, too!

Under the table, I politely untied
the ribbons

of my ugly American
ballet shoes.

Merci beaucoup.

Calling the Couturier to Come

———

Come measure me. I am not a standoffish thing.
I am waiting in the hotel salon, naked.
And my hair stands on end.
I am a satellite transmitting. I am a gift.

Delinquent, dress me in your just-past-midnight.
Call me your saint. Call me Immaculate.
The bat is kissing the glowworm.
And the owls know your name. I wait.

The barman checks in on me. The pianist
is murdering an Art Tatum tune.
Even through the wall, one can hear
she can really clear a room.

The barman gets an eyeful.

The Actress is Me, Briefly

———

The lie is exquisite.
She's swiped my life,
married herself to my tears
and husband,
buried her face in his coat, crying,
"Tell me I'm brave
and I will never leave you."
He doesn't say a word.
 (It's complicated.)
She does, of course, leave him,
but only long enough
to turn a steamy corner—
and then—what does she do?
She turns back! It *is* raining,
after all, and running in heels
is such a pain in the ass.

Credits roll; the lie desists.
Hubby and I cuddle up, and kiss.

The Bats

———

I heard them first, then turned and watched
the world's lost postcards
deliver themselves from one tree to the next.

They were efficient, organized, like good campers—
leaving behind dusk and silence
just as they'd found them.

Why did I feel so changed?

Did the sunset improve, the trees grow dearer,
the air shift in its seat?
For a minute, maybe.

It was like hearing you call my name, watching
you cross a dark room.
Cross my heart, it was just like that.

Divorce

———

The hammers we carried
the dents we made
the ceilings we collapsed
the bodies we buried
are yours and mine.

Like Brahms, Op. 39, no. 5 in E Major

———

Our love is full
of whispers and bells.

The whispers, kind and unkind,
have been told

and will tell

of our lives, our lives
bended together,

mended and broken
and mended again.

Together we waltz,
however fitfully,

to a tolling, a clock sound
transformed,

and the whispers—

the whispers
know what they know.

What I Have

———

A mind that occupies me,
and that I occupy.
My mind is my home.
It does not always have a fireplace.
Curtains do flutter, often.
There is a man there, and a little girl.
They write on the walls.

II
September 11, 2001

———

Paper sky, lightning sky, soot sky: red.
The sky is peopled with the dying and dead.

Sky in the morning, sky at nine AM.
The rueful sky is at indelicate ends.

A one-way corridor, privy with grief.
At nine AM, at nine oh three.

Lovely sky.

The Onions, the Flowers

———

I gather them up like children.

It's a perfect partnership;
they each serve
their purpose, have
a place
at the table.

It is not the same
with us. Of the same
deep earth,
we cannot drink
or eat
with one another,

having been raised
hillsides apart.

Underground

For relief workers everywhere

———

Few have received
what we have reciprocated.

Few, able-minded,
have looked to starlight,
the triumph of starlight,

and so, in the midst of this,
our revolution,
we are ashamed to hope.

Those who were born here
have never seen sky.
It is a rumor, like fruit.

And yet we sing,
as the stars have done.

Of life, though we have died,
though we are dying still.

Ghost at the Reading of the Will

———

My love is an offish red and wilted rose.
My love is a seasick green, kisser of toads.
My love is an armored truck, upended.
My love is a high wire act, stranded.
My love is a fox, sought after by hounds.
My love is a farce, sung in a round.
And this is its funeral. Hear them sing.
And hear them seek after worldly things.
And hear them squawk of what's befallen.
And watch the money blow like pollen.
And see them turn from my frigid cheek.
And how with each verse, the lawyer winks.

The Daughters of Danaos

———

Each maiden thus forced
to draw water from the well,

Felt upon her wedding night,
although you couldn't tell,

That much rather than be saddled,
she'd ride him down to hell,

Her husband caught by dagger
between the tail and the genitals.

Zombie

———

The streets are new, and I walk
with a new penny in my mouth, a new
beggar's kiss.

My eyes are not windows
from which I look out. My eyes are not mirrors.
You cannot call me by my Christian name.

But I do feel
some measure of devotion. Come here. I will lick you
clean as a cub.

I can smell your blood.

Horses

The crazy woman
in the crazy coat
with the crazy frog
in her crazy throat
is screaming about horses.

"Who took my horses?" to the barge on the lake,
churning on its foamy feet.

"Who took my horses?" to the workers at the mill,
all of them, hearts made of steel.

"Who took my horses?" to the railcars, the tracks,
the fanatical click and maniacal clack.

"Who took my horses?" to me on my way,
but I couldn't find them, or help her, or say.

Acidalia Planitia

———

Tell me what I've set forth
is but fit for the pasture
and I will shock you
with fertility.

I am Mars. Yet in me
there is life, little green
embryonic goldmines.

I've given myself up to—
(lousy criminal) Death.
For the space It lends
to life, astonishes.

And I am confident
you <u>will</u> inhabit me,
gossip-be-damned.

There is a newness about.
Springing forth from the last
grim heave of the sickle,
blue-green faced.

Humanness is the syn-
onym for the skeptic
hid in your only fault.

Tell me you'd rather be alien,
bizarre and in love with me
when I lead you to the
mysterious core.

We shall inhale-exhale
at once, immortal as
any good piece of work.

Lean closely to the stone.
Rivers are wagging mad
under that tuff.

The Ghost in My Prayer

———

When I was a girl, I kneeled down to pray
With a question, a coda, repeating:
Lord, what would you have me do on this day?
I fear from the depths, my will won't keep me.

I've studied. Daily, The Bible, I've searched,
Yet I don't know what it is I'm to do.
I've gone to my lessons, attended church,
Still a hunger, unrefined, has pursued.

Then, like an answer, came a gentle calm.
I rose from my knees, and got into bed.
A smile rose upon my mouth like a song.
Gone were my feelings of want and of dread.

But even in that warm, heavenly light,
An old foe, or old friend, came to meet me.
Through my door, he came—unnatural white,
And held me at the throat, and would not leave.

God Forgive Me

———

I slipped out
behind the church
because
I could not listen
one more minute
to the kind man
at the microphone.

God forgive me,
I heard a rushing
of leaves
and went out
in that unholy traffic
to play.

Mule

———

I want you the way a believer
wants a mule
on her way up the mountain
to the shrine.
Believing is easier
when you have a good ride.

Mallorca, Two Doors Down From 18-A

———

The music begins
and I am

on that rooftop again,

longing to do that hat-dance we did,

to see you as you were, figgy-limbed,
mouth like a thief's, stealing
its gems.

The light arms of laughter
are ours

without end. Four white fish,
hooked and sinkered,

glisten, even at the foot of the line.

Take your guitar from the corner; *La Castigada*
is punished enough.

*   *   *

The music begins
and I am

on that rooftop again,

longing to speak that we-speak we had,

to know you as you were, whimsy-legged,
mind like a staircase, winding
and mad.

The quick eyes of wonder
are girlhood's

and should be glad. Two bright limes,

caught and bottled,

shimmy, even at the bottom of The Gulf.

Piece them a song from the wreckage
they've known.

Marcela

———

Five years old, they drugged her up,
put her in a truck.
Officer said, "What a beautiful face."
No border *she* can't jump.

Thirty years later, I greet Marcela:
real estate agent.
We meet in San Antonio for lunch.
"Where are you from?" I ask.

She starts, "I don't remember much."

Oranges

———

I walk my daughter through the morning fog to school,
a bag of oranges in her hands.
I think: This is how she will keep entering life. This is how
she will move through its doors.
I bite my thumbnail until it bleeds, and suck on it a little
the lone way home.

The Meatpacker

———

She didn't look like the rest of us.
Her jeans were too nice.
In the plant's blue light, her hair
shone like ice.

Pale eyes pausing
on a block
of pink and darker pink, she turns.
Her little throat is a vein.

"Don't you think they look like dolls' hearts?"

Sally

———

Fiddle-dee-dee-faced, you were my first, Sally.
The mouse-brown braids, and wee, ironed-on mouth
must have fallen off by now.

I imagine those felt lips, old as mothballs,
awaiting some disembodied head, a bit of glue,
a thumb prick, stitch or two.

I took a ride in a mirrored elevator today, Sally.
My hair is perfect, but my mouth?—a lost element,
with no real say in this office place.

"You're such a doll," Greg says. *Greg!*

We've got to find our mouths again, Sally. We've got to!
We've got to stick together, me and you.

She Was

———

Grinding into shape—
Arranging by width and length—

The little scissors, clipping—
The reddish color, chipping—

Wearing silver shoes
that tap around the office building:

she was filing her nails.

15 Minutes

———

Finding a space
between wall and sky,
I strike a match

and sobbing, put it out
on the concrete.

What use is it
to go on lighting things?

If only in secret
fires start, and in corners
women sob,

no spark, no niche
is doing anybody
any good

at all.

Snake

How else can she love you
but with the unraveling skein
of her mind?

How else can she love you
but with the ferocious
biting on
of her mind?

How else can she love you
but by lying on the cool sand,
knowing the moon,
the mortality of the hawk,
and her own mortality?

These are your considerations
when she rolls over
and asks,

"*Psst*. Can you pass the ribs?"

My Moose, My Bear

You are not mine, and yet you snort in my ear
and claw at my heart.
You stomp through the moss of my mind.
Nuzzles and paws replace kisses and hands.
It is a lost world. I can claim nothing
but that I love you.

A Cracked Pot

———

That slumps on the sill
is at the mercy
of what grows from it still.

A Grown Man

———

Who sits on your stoop
is happy to watch
the kids playing hoop.

Wish

———

Carry me, Grandfather, like you did
the night I faked sleep
so that in your white-haired arms,
your Navy man's arms,
I'd be lifted from the car to the house
and with you a little longer.

Wrinkles

———

I don't have wrinkles yet,
but I know they're coming.
If I don't die tomorrow
or the next day or the next, they're coming.
They'll see me home.

From One Old Player to Another

———

Yours is a sad possession.
Look at her, crumbling at the bar,
wet as a newborn; she should be screaming.

She is an oyster in your mouth—crippled.
Your words are swollen, fallen fruit.

Come to me as a man, then, if you can possess so well.
Take me in her stead.

She is too young to understand

                              you aren't thinking with your head.

Break me like a chain. Take me at the neck.
I've earned my pearls. Your fat tongue is underdressed.

The Promise

———

Fondly, is how we said we'd think
of one another,
but what does that mean?

Does that mean I'll think of you
when my dishwasher is on the fritz?

Will you miss my little pom-poms
next time your ego takes a lick?

I'll think of you fondly,
we both promised,
but what does that mean?

It means I didn't care enough for you
and you didn't care enough for me.

When I Hear Violins

———

Birds in-
side the
wood and up-
on the
strings be-
gin to sing
you are a-
live and in the
wind a-
long the bows
I am a-
fright!

Under a Rock-n-Roll Moon

———

She who waxes and wanes like the paean
Regardless of the dogs, the chains, the moat,

Storms the castle I'd been keeping hid in,
Lullabies monkey-dancing in her throat

From which coyotes run and wail, scared
Through a cornucopia of hazard she swims,

Windpipe beating down on lock and lever,
Pulling a slow, even mantra from her limbs.

Wendy, at My Place

_____

When the day I've spooned up
is getting cold in the bowl,

and noon comes a harpy's call
(and not a bell or a chime at all),

and the night face, then so tired,
grows sicker still with yellow stars,

oh, friend, how fine and fortunate for me
that you show up. You are one hot cup!

You dance to the tune of life—Why else?—for fun.
"When you look to the universe," you tell me,

"at least your chin is up."

Karie and I Were Both Good Girls

_____

Still, we slipped off to the creek
in the middle of the day,
took off our shirts and splashed around
that way, cursing and telling little jokes.

It wasn't a real creek. It wasn't _dangerous_.
Only a few blocks from the house!

That's where I'd take off my blouse,
and she would, too,
and we'd splash, and curse, and tell little jokes.

Her Family Raised Georgia Peaches

———

They raised pecans, too—well, didn't raise them
So much as harvest them from a small grove
Where her brother liked to walk with girlfriends,
And where she had been forbidden to go.

The rest of the land was for the peaches,
That like her, were welcome all summer long
To cover three fourths of the farm's acres,
But then downright strong-armed at the pecans.

All her life, she'd been regaled with tall tales
Of Shakers long dead, shaking out evil,
And of young girls who could still hear them wail
Under the trees where they'd once kept vigil.

Tonight, she's fifteen, and she won't listen,
Sneaking out, unafraid, shoes in her hands,
To meet the boy she won't be caught kissing
Out on the back fourth, under the pecans.

Breathless

———

When I am older—an old woman,
I will think

on this moment.

I will think:

on my mouth
was once

the animal of his name.

The Necklace

———

I fell down in the churchyard grass
to search for the necklace I'd lost.
Every blade, from first to last,
I parted; each leaf, gently, I tossed.

For every stain I procured there,
I could not find the thing I loved.
Just as it was in The Church, where,
on dusted knees, I found no God.

I See the Lake for the First Time in Years

———

And suddenly I miss the earrings
my mother used to let me wear:

two gold starfish
that once belonged to my grandmother.
I lost one in the lake
after I was told to come in—no more swimming!

I remember I hoped it would be found
like Jonah

who returned from a library of gut
all the way to the shore
where his mother must have been
so happy to see him.

But no whales live in Lake Michigan.

They were pretty, the earrings.
I think my mother cried
when she saw that I'd lost one, but I can't be sure.

The Lie

_____

It has been very small,
quite shut up

like some terribly disfigured darling
kept locked alone in a cellar
next to peaches in overstuffed jars
where anyone would hate to go,
especially in winter,
to get those pickled ears and eyes.

Hear it?

It is trying to convince us it's a secret
but we know it is a lie.

I Love You, Philomena!

_____

What I didn't understand
is why he held onto my foot
when he knew
all day
I'd been scared of swimming
with the sky turned gray like that.

But he stopped me long enough
to let a wave crash at the back
of my neck, to fill
my mouth with saltwater.

He did the funniest thing, then. He shouted, "I love you, Philomena!"
My name is _not_ Philomena.

I don't take well to halting admissions of love, given any name.
I told him just, "Let go of my foot."

To Meagan, on Her Wedding Day

———

You were a dream once
of naked mouth and eyes, black and full
as the deepening pond out back.

I see you, Meagan, lunchbox by your side.
Every girl needs a capable clutch
(or badge-toting, blue-capped beaux, or some such—),
or some shiny thing upon which to decide.

You've grown up.

You were a dream once
of naked mouth and eyes, black and full
as the deepening pond out back.

Best wishes,

Aunt Ginny.

The Letter

———

There is a letter in the mail
which may require some explaining.
Thinking of it now, I go white,
and shrink. O hollow, dry, rotting thing!

Did I mean to cling like a burr
with my hooks and teeth to your heart?
No, I only meant to be heard,
which I hope this addendum imparts.

My Black Barbie Was the Maid

_____

She didn't have a name.
She was just the maid, my only black Barbie.

My black Barbie was the ugliest.

I dressed her in my oldest, tired Barbie clothes.
Otherwise, I didn't play with her much.
I forgot about her.

Ken used to kidnap my Barbies, one by one.
He did it from ugliest to prettiest. It was an honor to be kidnapped last.

Ken would hit all of them. Slap them in the face!

Black Barbie was lucky. Ken stole her first, and didn't hit her that much.
His best slaps were saved for the new and shiniest,
which makes sense.

Do you know anything about brothers?
Mine were ordinary scoundrels.
Bored one day, they burned my Barbies, one by one.

I'm so scared. I'm scared to know who they thought to burn first.
I'm scared to know who they thought to burn last.
I'm scared to know who they didn't bother to burn.

Maybe it's okay. Black Barbie wasn't a who.
Lucky girl: before my brothers got to her, I probably threw her away.

The Girl in the Painting

_____

She can only look down on me
and say what the silence can say:
that neither of us, seeming free,
are free, being framed, in our way.

The Hammer

———

Crack, pow, crack!

The fence is coming along.
I am building it for you, daughter,
knowing one day I'll have to turn this hammer around,
unplug the nails I'm plugging in now,
let the world in, and let the world(s) in you, out.

Crack, pow, crack!

In you, my daughter,
in our daughters' daughters,
and so on, I have no doubt.

The Cloud

———

It's moved on, or dissipated,
the way people do, the cloud over his house.

The truck in the drive
is no longer in the drive.
His lover is gone.

The child's bicycle
that had status on the porch,
has disappeared.

It didn't take long.
It happened in the space of a song.

He misses the cloud, benevolent, unsound,
and the truck,
and the bike,
the song.

Why does the old man smile?

While Abroad

I once stayed with a woman
who taped a black thread
to her baby's forehead.

I asked why. – To stop a cough.

She put a half-glass of water
beneath her baby's bed.

I asked why. – To catch the bad.

Two days later, the baby,
gurgling, bright-eyed,
was kicking, spitting, smiling.

He was *laughing*!

Did you go to the doctor?
Of course! the woman said.
Do you think me mad?

The thread, the water, the doctor—
THE MOTHER

stopped the cough,
caught the bad.

Pearls

Brighter than her smile,
the string of ocean-fruit at her throat.

She calls to him, "Good-bye!" her body
half out the BMW.

She wasn't trying to be cruel
to the chap without wheels.

She was merely waving the wave
a certain girl can give

when she's in one man's convertible
and another man's pearls.

Furball

———

Arguing
on the way to Colorado,

nowhere near
Amarillo—is this how it's going to go?

Then, smack! The fender takes a hit.

We pull over
to find the silver, the red
fur
laid out like an inkblot.

From Childress to Denver, we say nothing
of the argument we had before,

reminded that some things, ripped
apart,

can't be put back together,

no matter how sad,
no matter how sorry.

If We Could Break the Flesh Honorably

_____

If we could break the flesh honorably

would our bodies be holy together
as they are alone?

Would we be so enamored
with these, our precious cocoons?

Could we baptize one another, in one
another's skins?

Less lonely, for this sweet and sullen
devotion.

Bored at Church

_____

I count the beams on the ceiling.
One, two, three, four, five, six, seven—who cares?

I invent a fairy. That's better.
She is a wild thing! She's tiny, as fairies usually are,
and a chameleon of sorts. Her skin changes color
with her mood. When she's bored, she's all the more
colorful. She's also up to no good.

She dances on the podium during testimonies.
She sticks her tongue out like that dude from the band Kiss.
Her gestures are obscene, but super funny.

If anyone else in the chapel could see her, they'd flip.

Amen! It is finally time to go home.
I resolutely flit to the family station wagon.

Next week, I'll invent a gnome.

You, Everywhere

———

Walking the stone beach at dawn
I see a small cliff

and make out, between the coalescing
and yanking waves,

your face in the rock. Love watches from a lighthouse,
and blinks.

And again, in the Czech bakery's
pastry case

among the sweetbreads, a loose cherry
on the parchment

is your mouth. Love rots in me like a tooth, I have known
such sweetness.

Over the hill, the old house sits
and it is you

on the swing, holding your guitar
like a child,

singing to it like a child. It is only morning, and already
you are everywhere.

About the author:

Bronmin Shumway lives with her husband and daughter in Chicago, IL. She is the winner of a handful of literary awards, including The Austin Poetry Society Award. *The Night You Were Born* is her first full-length collection of poems.

www.ingramcontent.com/pod-product-compliance
Lightning Source LLC
Chambersburg PA
CBHW021338140626
46545CB00020B/2848